The Source to Life

Life Source Scholars

Grades 6 -9

The Source to Life

Written by the scholars of Life Source International Charter school grades 6-9 May 2017.

Published by:
Affirmative Expression
PO Box 360856
Decatur, GA 30036

First edition copyright © 2017, Affirmative Expression

All rights reserved. No part of this book may be reproduced or transmitted in any form or by any means, electronic or mechanical, including photocopying, recording, or by any information storage or retrieval system, without written permission of the author.

Cover by Chelsey Thomas
chels.t14@gmail.com

Printed in the United States of America

ISBN: **978-0-9963605-5-5**

Letter from the Publisher

The Anthology Project is a program created to provide a platform for voices to be heard. Often times youth feel their voices are not valuable. Others may feel pressure from the concern of their work being good enough for a passing grade. But while participating in this collaborative project they are able to speak freely with no concern for whether they will pass or fail. Most importantly, through the support of readers like you, their voices, stories, and efforts are validated and for that I thank you.

Tierica Berry
CEO
A Woman's Standard

FOREWORD

When I created the Anthology Project it was to shed light on the voice of today's youth as it relates to various topics. Over the past few months I have had the honor and pleasure of working with the scholars of Life Source International Charter School.

These scholars were asked about the keys to success. During dialogue about this topic they were able to come together and write this book:

The Source to Life

Enjoy.

♥

Tierica Berry

CONTENTS

Ms. Maritz Pg 3

Ms. Correa Pg 33

Mr. Berman Pg 79

Ms. Grose Pg 97

ACKNOWLEDGMENTS

Before we begin special thanks must be giving to the people that made this anthology project possible.

Dr. Culpepper for seeing the vision and bringing the Anthology Project to Life Source.

Mr. Mix because under his guidance the project has been steered in the right direction.

The front office staff **Ms. Powers, Ms. Padilla, and Ms. Lopez** for helping to manage some of the fine details of this project.

Mr. Howard for assistance in scheduling.

Mrs. Mix for planning the book signing.

Last but certainly not least special thanks to the classroom **teachers** that worked closely with the scholars to complete their writing submissions. Without you this book would not be possible.

On behalf of Affirmative Expression and the student authors,
Thank You!

CHAPTER 1

MS. MARITZ

Definition of Success

My definition of success is gaming and soccer because it's the best. Messi the famous soccer player is my hero. My famous gamer is Jack Sepiteye because he is cool. I think success means to do what you believe in like your goal and dream. Success if you're doing something you believe in. If you don't like basketball you don't have to play it. My goal is to be a soccer player and a gamer because it's fun to play. Basketball may be also but I don't know. The challenges I might face are objects and laps and other stuff for soccer. Gaming is easy to learn if you're good at it. The thing I might overcome is eating healthy. The scary part is when you have to play in soccer games.

Brian
Male
6th Grade

My Definition of Success

My definition of success is when you achieved a goal. My goal is to get into the WNBA. Some challenges I may face are getting injured, losing games, and being talked about. I can deal with these challenges by icing and getting medical treatment for my injuries. When I lose games I can go practice and find my mistakes. If I am being talked about I have to disregard what's being said about me unless it is constructive criticism.

Anonymous
Female
6th Grade

My Definition of Success

My definition of success is to become a basketball player. I love basketball. Basketball is my favorite sport. When I was little and I sprained my ankle. I was scared when I did that. That was my fear. I overcame that fear. I never want to give up my dream. I think success means to accomplish your dreams. Like my sister wanted to accomplish her dream and she did. I'm so proud and happy for her. My family is proud of her also. I gave my sister ice cream when she got a 100% on her test. My sister said she will never give up. My goal is to be a basketball player. Basketball is my life. I would like to focus on basketball more. I try my best when playing basketball. I never want to give up on basketball. When I get pushed on the basketball court I get right back up. The challenges I might face is that trying to get the rebound for example, when I'm trying to make a shot. It's kind of hard to play defense on a taller person. I try my hardest. One day, I was playing basketball and I was tired and sore. I felt like quitting.

Tiarrah
Female
6th Grade

Success Means...

I think success means ways to find ways to solve problems. Success helps your earn a degree and get the job you want. Success can help you succeed in life. If you don't have success you can become a homeless person on the street. In conclusion, education is the path to success.

My dream in life is to become a veterinarian and study animals. I want to become a veterinarian because I have dog that has a hurt leg and the veterinarian can not fix his leg. My second reason is I had a dog that walked funny and he was just suffering, so we went to put my dog to sleep. Also, my dream to become a veterinarian can help prevent animals from passing away. In the end, I can help families stay happy with their best friend.

The challenges I might face becoming a veterinarian are that I might not be able to cure the animal. I can overcome this obstacle by studying and asking other veterinarians who have cured animals for help. Another obstacle that I might face is I might be too sad for the animal and not want to help the animal. For this obstacle I can learn that most animals will be close to dying. Finally, success can get you to where you want to be when you're older.

M.G.
Female
6th Grade

My Goals

One of my goals is to help the homeless. I want to help those people out because some people just think of them as nobody. Also, I think if I do this I will be blessed at the same time their getting blessed. I will help the homeless by getting them a homeless shelter to live in. This might be more helpful to the homeless if more people participate in this activity.

Another goal of mine is getting a great education so my family can be proud. I won't get an education just for my family, but I will have to get if for myself. Also, I will need an education in life for almost everything. In life you need an education for many things like to get a good job, to work for someone, to do a certain skills, like engineering you need to be good at math. This is why I intend on continuing my education.

Challenges I might face to help the homeless is proving the resources they need, like food and water. Another challenge I might face is building the shelter by myself. My other goal is to make my family proud by getting an education a challenge I might face is needing to study hard. I might not get much me time if I am always studying. These are my goals and challenges. What's yours?

J.E.P.
Female
6th Grade

My Goals

    My career goal is to be a cosmetologist. I will work my toward being a cosmetologist by graduating elementary. I will work my way up to high school and graduate there. Furthermore, I will go and really work my way up as a college graduate and get my cosmetology degree. I think I will go to Paul Mitchell Beauty School.

    The challenges I might face are not being able to please the customers. When I'm in college might face the challenge of not finishing my work or staying up late. In addition, I might face the challenge of paying my way through school.

    I will overcome my challenges by making my customers happy. Also, I'll overcome them by finishing my work and not staying up late. I can overcome my challenges by getting a good job to pay off my tuition. I think success means when you do good, and get good grades to graduate college or high school. However, success can mean where you succeed and graduate from college and get a degree.

Aniya
Female
6th Grade

The Key to Success

I think the key to success means that if you want to accomplish something just do it and see what happens. If feels good to have success. Success is real and you can have it if you try your hardest at whatever your goal is. I'm going to to talk about my goals and dreams. I hope you like my dreams and goals.

My goal is to become a famous YouTuber. YouTube is a really big company and I hope to be on there soon. Being a YouTuber is way harder than you think. Firstly, you have to make the video. Secondly, you have to edit the video. Lastly, you have to publish the video, which may not be that hard as single goals, but all of that together will take a long time.

My last goal is to become a director at a young age. I already know how to film. I just don't know how to edit yet. I really want to film a movie and maybe somebody that works at a move development company of some sort will recognize it. I also need to film my YouTube videos. Both of these jobs involve filming and editing.

J.P.
6th Grade

Success Means…

When I'm older I want to become a YouTuber. The reason I want to be a Youtuber is because it is fun. It can actually become a job. It makes good money. It's nice to do something you love.

Success means doing accomplishments. It means doing something you love. Doing what you love makes gold.

I might face problems. My challenge could be getting hacked. I could get robbed. My channel could die.

Diego
Male
6th Grade

My Goals

My goals are to be an artist and to be an artist I have to practice and get colors. I really like art. It's been really fun. I love art.

My second goal is to be a dancer. I have to practice and try my best. I want to be a choreographer, and try to do my best to keep up.

Elizabeth
Female
6th Grade

Goals and Dreams

My goal is to be a professional artist because I like to draw and I like color. I would like to be a professional soccer player. The challenges I might face are getting hurt in soccer, and also people talking about my art and they are trying to hurt me by telling me it is ugly. I also might have to face the challenges that might have to face.

My dream is to be a professional artist, and I also want to be a professional soccer player. I also dream about succeeding in all my dreams. I hope that my dreams come true in art and being a soccer player. My other dream is when I grow up I want to build a shelter for the homeless doggies and a shelter for the homeless.

Justin
Male
6th Grade

My Goals

My goal is to be a professional soccer player. In order to be a soccer player I have to work on passing the ball and to make a goal. I also have to learn to do what I have to do in order to be good at it. I also can make my goal by studying what I want to accomplish.

The challenges I might face are responsibility, working, studying, helping, doing work, and doing a lot of stuff. I will overcome them by working hard on my studies and my life.

My other goal is to be a lawyer. To be a lawyer you have to study hard and work hard to be a lawyer. And also I have to get a diploma, probably 2-3 of them. To be a lawyer one has to do their best.

-Gabriela
Female
6th Grade

My Goal

My goal is to be a pro skater. First I want to be a SLS champion. I need to practice. Second, I need to produce videos and get recognized. I would have to get sponsored. The challenges I would face is needing money for boards. I would also need to be safe so I don't get hurt and I need be careful not to snap my board. I would need good health insurance. I need to invest in quality gear. It will be difficult to travel and attend school. I need to have the resources. Lastly, I may get homesick while traveling. I need to have enough shoes. I need to work very hard.

-Anonymous
6th Grade

My Goal

My goal is to enter team Barcelona and become the next Lionel Messi. My short term goal is to keep attending soccer practice until I'm an adult. If I enter to get scouted I want to get a pro contract. I think it's easier to get scouted to La Liga Santander (Barcelona's League). Then I have to learn a different dialogue for Spanish. The challenges that can come to me are be a pro by training every day to be like Lionel Messi. Traveling will be a hard challenge to achieve. I will have to leave my family but eventually I will visit them. I can overcome this challenge by making good money and giving my mom a ticket to fly to the country I will be in.

-Anonymous
6th Grade

My Goal

My goal is to become a hairstylist. I want to be a hair stylist because I like doing my sisters hair and I like learning from my older sister. I also want to be a hairstylist because I like doing designs in my sister's hair. I also like doing hair because I like for other people's hair to look good. My challenge will be finishing school and getting my degree. My third challenge is to go to beauty school and pass. My fourth challenge is to get better and better. Lastly, my challenge will be to start my own business. Another goal is to become a teacher as well. I want to be a teacher because I like teaching my little sister.

-Anonymous
6th Grade

My Goal

I want to be in the NBA or NFL because I want my family to be rich for generations and not have to struggle. To be in one of those leagues is not for the money but to give people what they. Some of the money will be for me to build a homeless shelters with workers getting paid enough. I will make sure it have showers, a cafeteria, a school for kids, a library, bathrooms, and nursery room. Before I do this, I have to go to college. I will need support from my parents to help me. . My other goals are to get people off the streets asking for food and to support them. I will have to overcome a lot of challenges in my life but if I don't get a scholarship I might not have enough money to go. I also might make an animal shelter because I love animals. My short time goals is to get through school

-Anonymous
6th Grade

The Definition of Success

My definition of success is accomplishing a goal or anything in life. To reach success I might have to follow my short term goals. Then follow your long term goals. Lastly I will need to go to school or practice depending on what I want to be. In conclusion, just follow your goals and or dreams and you get where you want to be. My goal is to become a lawyer. I am going to have to go through a lot of schooling. I would have to go through 4 years of college. Then 4 years of practicing. Lastly I want to become a lawyer. My challenges would be attending school. I would have to learn to be a lawyer and handle cases. I will overcome these challenges by staying in school and paying attention in all my classes.

-Anonymous
6th Grade

The Definition of Success

My definition of success is becoming an ultrasound technician because I like helping people. I know it's going to be hard work. It's like being a pediatrician. That is why I want to be an ultrasound technician. Another goal is to become a track star because it's my favorite sport. It keeps me active. It also helps me focus on running and staying fit. That's my goal to accomplish. My challenge to become an ultrasound technician and track start will be a challenge because it's hard work. I may also face injuries during track practice. I may also face a challenge getting during track meets and eating healthy.

-Anonymous
6th Grade

The Definition of Success

My definition of success is your dreams and your goals. My dreams and goals are to be a gymnast and track runner. I'm a pretty fast runner, and I am very good at gymnastics, so my goal or "key to success" is gymnastics and being a runner.

There are many good "keys to success", but there are also many struggles, and challenges you have to face, and pass through, like competitions and you lose if you don't have faith.

There are challenges of gymnastics. You can break your leg. You may mess up your playing or lose.

-Anonymous
6th Grade

The Definition of Success

I think success means to accomplish my goals. I want to be a doctor. I will have to go through a lot of school. 14 years of school. I want to do surgeries on people to make them feel better. I want to be a doctor because I want to help people not be sick any more. I want to by my mother's and father's doctor.

My challenge is going through a lot of school to learn how to do different kinds of surgery. I have to learn how to do a lot of stuff. I have to work really hard and making sure that I don't mess up on stuff. I have to make sure nobody dies in the operation room.

To overcome my challenges I have to overcome going to a lot of school by breaking your long time into short time. To overcome different kinds of surgery, I have to wake up early.

-Anonymous
6th Grade

My Dream

My dreams are to be a doctor in life. Being a doctor pays you good money. I chose this job for my life so I can help people who are sick or are in any kind of emergency. Since when I was little I would play doctor. I love to help people or animals. If I want to be a vet, then I need to study a lot.

My goals are my homework, my work, reading, and math. To accomplish these goals I should focus on my work, and work harder to achieve them. I will achieve these goals by challenging myself. If I work harder on my goals I will get a good education to get A's and B'. I want to work hard and study hard to pass and to have a good education, and good life, and a good job.

My definition of success is to succeed with my work and homework. I think success means to succeed in your work or something that you want to accomplish. I want to succeed at my job to earn money and get a house in the future when I grow up and I want to challenge myself by working hard in classes and getting a good education.

-Anonymous
6th Grade

My Goal

My goal is to go to the NBA. I got inspired by Steph Curry. He is a good basketball player. I also want to go to college. If I do make it to the NBA I will give my family and friends tickets to come. I take a good record to get in the NBA.

The challenges will be people telling me, "You'll never make it", but I think I will make it because I am a good kid. I have some bad grades. I have a lot of good ones. I can fix those grades. It is only my reading and writing. I know I have very good grades and I know I'm doing good.

There is another way I can get to the NBA. There are people called scouts that watch you on the court or in university. You have to be careful because they see your grades and they see how you act. They even watch you on the streets too. You also want to finish your classes too. Those are my goals.

The definition of success is when you beat something, like you pass a test or when you beat a level on a game.

-Anonymous
6th Grade

My Goal

For my first job I would like to make anime. I do this by drawing anime characters. I want to make anime because I love watching it. Being an anime designer would be a dream come true because I love seeing the faces of the sketches and the drawings in general. Those are the reasons why I would like to be an anime creator.

The next job I want is as a game developer. I can have this by having more creativity. If I make games I will make them different types of games. I decided to do this job because I love games. That is why I want to make games.

-Anonymous
6th Grade

My Success

My success is being an NBA star. I want to be a professional like my father. Success is *who* you want to be in life, and *how* you reach it. My goal is trying my best to help my mom, brother, and sisters. When I get older I want to help by paying her bills and give her a dream car. I want to keep going to college until I get an MA degree.

My next success is being an engineer. I want to work with cars , like Lamborghini or Ferraris. I would also like to test the car out to see how fast they go. I would like to keep learning math for engineering to see what part go in which. I want to work with building engines and the wheels. My favorite thing about cars is seeing the car go fast.

My challenges will be in the NBA. However, my defense is to practice more. My challenge in engineering is figuring out what tools to use and how to fix a car. My challenge for my mom is cleaning the entire house.

-Anonymous
6th Grade

The Definition of Success

My definition of success is to accomplish things to be successful. My goal is to be a pediatrician. I want to be a pediatrician because I want to help all the sick kids. I have to go through a lot of school. I have to go to college for four years and medical school for another four years.

Next, I believe that being a pediatrician can be lot of hard work. One of the challenges is waking up early. Also, another challenge of being a pediatrician is going to school for a long time. Another challenge of being a pediatrician is having to be there on time. The last challenge of being a pediatrician is making the kids stop crying because they are sick.

Lastly, the ways I can overcome these challenges are by going to sleep very early and waking up early. The challenge of going to school for a long time can be overcome by breaking long term goals intro short term goals. I can overcome going to work on time by getting ready fast and picking my clothing the night before. Finally, I can make the kids stop crying by telling them it is going to be okay, and by giving them candy.

-Anonymous
6th Grade

The Definition of Success

When I grow up my goal is to be a NFL player, I want to be NFL player because Carn Newton inspired me. Mostly because the way he played. He once said to never give up on your dream. Also, he said "Who cares what other people think. Do what you want to do. Don't let other people control you."

If becoming a NFL player doesn't work, then I will want to be a mechanic because my dad's a mechanic and it is interesting to help him. Also, if a car breaks down I can help and fix it. I can become a mechanic by going to vocational school and helping my dad. When I graduate I'm going to Firestone.

The challenges of being a NFL player is you will get hit alot, and get tackled. Or, you can get hurt like a broken leg or a concussion. The challenges of a mechanic is that stuff could fall on you. You could get cut or bruised and a finger could get cut off.

-Anonymous
6th Grade

My Goals

My goal is to be a better tether ball player. I want to be a champion at tether ball . I want champions to go against me, and then when I win I will be super happy that I won against a champion.

The challenge is that I want all the champions to go against me so when I win I will be a champion. After I beat all the champions, I will now be the master of tetherball.

My other goal is to be better at basketball because I'm not that good at shooting hoops. I sometimes make it, but sometimes I don't make it.

-Anonymous
6th Grade

The Definition of Success

What success means to me is hard work and opportunity. To be ready for life you can't do anything without success. You need to be able to get jobs so you can provide food for your family. Every time you got good grades just know success is waiting, so go get it.

My dream is to be an NBA player. How I'm going to be an NBA player is practice. My plan is to be finished paying for school, then to be noticed and play for AV High School and get noticed. I will play for a college, then I will be an NBA player.

Some of the challenges I'm going to face are injuries and not having a healthy body. However, the way I'm going to overcome them. A challenge breaker to get a healthy body is by eating vegetables, fruit, and drinking water. To overcome injuries I will need to play by the rules so I won't get hurt, and just make sure I try your hardest and have fun.

-Anonymous
6th Grade

The Definition of Success

My definition of success is to accomplish what you want to do as your goal. Nobody can stop you from your goal. Nobody can stop you from doing it. You can control your life. The Life Source Creed says to do what you want. Follow your dreams.

My goal is to become an artist, or vet because I like animals and because I like drawing and art. Practicing is good. You need to start now. If you start now, you will succeed.

My challenge is to take care of animals right now. To have practice for a vet. I will do what I have to do to succeed in life.

-Anonymous
6th Grade

CHAPTER 2

MS. CORREA

March 1, 2022

Dear future Arrieonna,

    I'm here to talk to you and give you a few tips on what to do in order to accomplish your goals and what I hope you have accomplished so far. Well, I hope you have achieved some of your goals because you are only 22, and that's pretty young. I hope you graduated from a college of your choice. If you did I'm very proud of you. I encourage you to still pursue your dream of becoming a lawyer. I know you are currently in law school and you are about to graduate and it's getting harder keep going. And to be successful you need to be committed to achieving this goal. You have to go to all your classes on time, and turn in your assignments on time. And in order to still become a seismologist you need to ace your studies and work very hard. I know you might be having issues with your family, and ya'll might disagree at times but in order to become successful you need to talk about your issues, talk civilly. Another thing you can do is pray. Pray that things will get better. And don't get discourage and keep going you will get far.

    I know you have many goals. Like I know you want to become a lawyer. Becoming a lawyer is a satisfying job but I know you have more you want to be in life like becoming a seismologist. You want to predict tsunamis, earthquakes, and other natural disasters. You want to do this because you want to keep people safe. Do not quit. Keep going. Although you have graduated from a four year college, you have to go back for a couple of years so you can get your master's degree. There will be some roadblocks. It won't just be an easy and smooth ride to accomplish your goals. Life isn't that easy, ask previous lawyers or seismologist. They will be sure to give you some great advice as I'm about to give you know.

    Alright now the topic that will help you in life. Learning your roadblocks and how to overcome them. Now, in law school you might have to do a debate with one of your classmates. And you might lose and it might bring down your confidence. Don't be discouraged. Keep trying, practice more. In life you don't always win, but don't give up, keep on going. Or say you have a major disagreement with your family don't get upset, just try to find a solution. Being a seismologist won't always be a piece of cake. Like your prediction might be wrong or something might go wrong. Don't fret, keep trying. Please accomplish all your goals. I hope you take these tips and use them to help you on your journey to success.

Sincerely Arrieonna

From March 2, 2017

Good Luck

-Arrieonna
Female
7th Grade

The Source to Life

February 28, 2017

Dear future Angel Arizmendi,

   Hello! How are things in the future? I hope everything is fine. In 2017, so far everything is good. I know how hard it is in the future people try to bring you down. I will tell you three things that are important.

   First, I will define what success is for you in case you forget. Success is to complete something you wanted to complete. Success is the best thing in life that you can ever do. Right now I will tell you that you be successful. Success is what you will be if you at least try because those who are not trying you are way ahead of them. You are going to look forward to success. There is no elevator to success only stairs to success.

   But, there will be roadblocks that try to bring you down. Roadblocks are people or other things that get in your way. There will be people who will make you feel like you can't reach your goal. There will be trouble, money problems, and the past or future. Maybe also your friends or family. You might do the wrong thing and go to jail, then your goals will be screwed.

   I saved the best for last your goals. Your goals are to graduate from UCLA. Get a degree but the highest of them all. Try to look for a soccer team that is available then join that team I will try to join at the age of 26. Lastly be an artist at the age of 30 then you will share that money that is on the street.

Love,

Angel from 2017

A.A.E.
Male
7th Grade

What I Feel Success Is

Success to me, is overcoming a challenge,

Achieving your goals and most importantly being happy.

Your goals encourage you to do something amazing.

You want to travel and meet new people.

Graduate college and become a writer.

With all these goals you are going to accomplish

There are going to be challenges.

People are going to make you feel small,

Put you down, and make you feel like you can't

Accomplish anything.

Stay strong and never give up.

You are smart and I know you can do whatever

You put your mind to.

Prove to everyone who said, "You can't do it" wrong.

Prove that you can, because I know you can.

-Chantel
Female
7th Grade

Dear Au'Jhanae,

Success is to me achieving something. To KNOW YOUR GOALS. You won't be successful if you don't know what you're going to do in life. You have to go to school and get your education so you can be whatever you want to be in life. You have to KNOW YOUR GOALS. If you want to be in the NBA or the NFL, they don't take straight F students or D's and C's and F's. Those are all bad grades so it's better to get A's and B's and focus on school and your career. Sooner in life you have to get a college degree but just don't drop out of Middle school, High school, or College.

My goal is to graduate Middle school, go through High school like it was nothing (graduate also) then go to college and study law. Then go to law school and get my master's degree in law school. Then I will become a lawyer and work on family cases like divorces and sending people to prison. That is my dream and maybe it is not yours but it is your decision.

A few roadblocks that might stop you from achieving your goal are maybe your grades because not everybody gets perfect grades and money and you have to get through HS without getting into fights or getting held back because it can mess up your record and get you in trouble. Drugs is also a roadblock because they can mess up your mind and cause you to have a sickness. It will also cause you to get distracted. I you want to be a sports player and be a success in sports, you can't be in any if you take drugs and it's also against the law. So all I'm telling you to do is go to school and NEVER GIVE UP ON ANYTHING.

Sincerely,

Au'Jhanae

-Au'Janae
Female
7th Grade

The Source to Life

February 28, 2017

Dear Caiou in 2017,

This is Caiou, but in the future. We are now 18 and attending the University of Duke. I want to give you some tips to stay on track. You have a long journey so I am going to help you be successful in life. These are some keys to success.

Success is to accomplish your goals. Also I know you want to be rich so you have to be successful. Success is also doing something you like to do. Also, I know you have to work hard to be successful. You have to have goals to reach so you can be successful.

Even though we made it to college doesn't mean stop working hard and forget about your goals. I know you want to go to Duke so you have got to keep working. Also I know you want to go in get a degree. If you want to be rich and have mansions, and be in the first round pick of the NBA, and become a professional, you have to be successful. You have to work hard to accomplish these goals. But remember there will always be some roadblocks in your life.

Here are some roadblocks that can interfere with your goals. You can maybe get hurt or injured permanently. Or you don't get a scholarship because you are not working hard. Also your grades can drop and you will get kicked out of the school. So I will give you some tips to overcome these roadblocks.

Stretching can help with getting hurt because your bones will be flexible. For scholarships you just have to work hard, compete, and get noticed. For the grades just study and do all of your work and be focused. These are all of the tips have for you so sink it into your brain. The rest is on you, what you are going to do in your life, you're either going to succeed or fail.

Don't give up,

Caiou

Caiou
Male
7th Grade

July 4, 2022

Dear 13-year-old Chanay,

Hey, we are in the 12th grade and we are going to Duke. We got a scholarship! We worked hard to get there. Now I need to remind you what to do as a 13-year-old. You need to keep working hard in school and in basketball.

Our goals in life are to finish college. Another one of our goals are to make it to the WNBA. Also our goal is to have money. Another one of our goals is to meet LeBron James. Also to meet Candace Parker.

Some roadblocks we face in life are waking up for school. More roadblocks are you're not always going to want to go to practice. Also more roadblocks are to get a job in college.

LOVE,

18-year-old Chanay

-Chanay
Female
Th Grade

Dear future us,

Make your haters into motivators, get them grades and make straight A's.

So one of your goals in life is to reach the top,

Become the best and don't listen to the mess.

Success is to me the most powerful key,

Good career and be happy and make yo' money.

Slay all day and don't worry what these haters got to say.

"Motivation is what gets you started, habit is what keeps you going."

Knowing your goals can be the first key follow these instructions carefully.

Go to college, get your degrees and become something.

Be famous; be rich live your life happily.

Becoming a lawyer: becoming a dancer knowing your goals is the only answer.

At the end of the day, challenges will come, but it's okay don't worry

Because you can overcome them.

But don't get too caught up because that's when doors with no keys will come.

Inside these doors there are people, work, and even yourself.

The only person that lets you in is you

but you can dodge it if you know those things will not sabotage you.

Love,

Deonne and Samaria

                             -Malia Samaria Rose Love   *- Deonne*
                                                          Female   Female
                                                       7th Grade 7th Grade

February 28, 2017

Dear D'Andre in 2022,

How are you? Success means first, I have got to get good grades. Then, I got stay out of trouble before I can get to college. But I have to make sure that they accept me first.

My goals are that I have to make sure that I don't get injured. My goals are that I make myself to go Ohio State so that I can get my college degree and then get drafted into the NFL. So that I can play for the team that I like: The Cowboys.

The roadblocks to my goals will be to pass high school. Then when I am done with high school. I can focus on college because that's the key to success. I got to focus on good grades, making money for my family, and helping others that don't have it.

Sincerely,

D'Andre

-D'Andre
Male
7th Grade

The Source to Life

February 28, 2017

Dear Future Dominic,

Wassup future me? Let's talk about how to accomplish goals, Dominic. Success means achieving something that you want to accomplish- something that is good for your life.

Dominic, remember your goals are to be an NFL player. Also, to get good grades and stay in school.A nd don't forget the only thing holding you back is yourself. The things that are keeping you from being a NFL player are your grades and you can't let yourself hold yourself back. Your grades can't be lower than 2.0 Noooo!!!!!!!!!!! It has to be 4.0. That's your goal to be an NFL player. Your next goal is to have good grades and graduate. But the only thing holding you back is you. You can't let you hold you back. Remember, stay on track and focus.

Sincerely,

Dominic Traylor

-Dominic
7th Grade

Feb 28, 2017

Dear Leroy,

How are you doing? What is the future like? To me success means everything good. But to have success is having goals to accomplish and somewhere to be in life. But to have success you have to have discipline. But most people do not have discipline. To have success you have to also have to respect one another. I know Leroy that you can be kind to people. I know that you have a nice car, house, and wonderful wife.

Leroy, I know your goals in life are to get a nice car, house and to have a job and some kids. I also would like to get in a nice company enough to pay all of my rent. I would like to be traveling with my family to new places. I would like to get a good education so I can have a clean record. I would like to go work out with my big brother.

So what can help me is to stay to myself and do not worry about others. I can also call my family if I ever need help. I know that the roadblocks cannot mess with me ever. All I need to do is be alone, achieving success which is an important part of life. So with this one body i am going to find a way to overcome challenges and achieve success.

Sincerely,

Leroy

-L.B.
Male
7th Grade

Success Poem

Success
Something good will happen
Like achieving a goal
Or overcoming a challenge

What are your goals?
Please tell me
If I don't know
How will I be helping?

Roadblocks
They may be hard
But if you overcome them
You will go far

Shoot for the moon
Land on a star
Drive a nice car
Go live on mars

How to overcome them
That's hard to say
If you have roadblocks
Try hard anyway

Get a job
Go to school
Education
Is cool

If you can't
That's alright
Just try
With all your might

Success is key
That's on me
If you don't
Just wait and see!

-Jaiya
Female
7th Grade

The Source to Life

February 14, 2018

Dear future me,

Hi! This is Leilany from 2017 and I am in 7th grade. I will tell you about success. To me success is that you don't stop thinking what you want to do with your career. You have to be a happy person and a smart person if you want to get through life. If you drop out of high school you might be a homeless person and you want to get a great job. One of my friends wants to be known for something good and that is very successful.

My goals right now are selling one of my drawings since I draw and earn some money. I would like that this year I do not get into drama or trouble because I hate to get in trouble because it gives my mom more work. My most important goal is to become a good artist. I really want to stop being lazy because it is bad for me I want to go outside play a sport. I want to get into a really good college so I can get a good life and job.

Some of the roadblocks I will have are not going to the right college. I might not get info time to study and get kick out of school. Might hang out with the kids and get into lots of trouble. I can become a lazy person and stay in the house all day.

Sincerely,

Leilany

-Leilany
Female
7th Grade

My Definition of Success

Success to me is, achieving my goals, being recognized for something good, and being happy; living happily. Success is something you should be proud of. Success, just a happy word; with success you can reach the top of your own little mountain. You got this don't give up!

My goals are important to me. My goals are to graduate high school, go to an amazing   university, meet different people, have a good family, and my favorite is to become a famous doctor. If i can do it you can do it too. So my goals are very special to me only.

Roadblocks and challenges are in life. Yes, there are many different types of struggles.   Some of my roadblocks could be haters, distractions, bad influence on me, I might not have enough money, or even getting into a really bad school. Although i doubt myself easily and give up easily I will still try my best.

Overcoming roadblocks and challenges can be difficult, but it can be easy at the same time. Just imagine going into a great school and turning all those grades into straight amazing A's. So don't doubt yourself just do what's right. For example, if you do not have enough money earn it do your part. So you got this reach success.

-Samantha
Female
7th Grade

The Source to Life

February 28, 2017

Dear Makaila in 2030,

I know as you grow older you define success a little differently but as your younger self, I am telling you now that my definition of success is, being happy. Being happy is key #1. If you're not happy how are you going to be successful? My other definition of success is to accomplish my goals, your goals may be different from mine because you are way older than I am but no matter what, still accomplish your goals. You're awesome and don't let anyone kill your awesomeness. My other definition of success is having a good career. So, how are you going to be successful?

As your younger self you have already accomplished some of our goals but to remind you, these are my goals. First off, I want to become an astronomer and study stars because that is my enjoyment in life. Secondly, I want to be 100% happy I know in my heart if I am not happy I am not going to be successful, but I hope you are happy more than anything. Third, I want to travel to a lot of places. I want to go to Florida and see a lot of plants and see brand new things people have never seen before.

Now, as your younger self telling you I don't like people telling me I am horrible at something or I can't do it. Also there will be plenty of people trying to tell you to just give up and don't even try. There will also be plenty of hate letters if you become famous and they will hurt you to read them. They will be very hurtful because people are writing very mean things about you in a letter. There will also be payments of stuff and you might not be able to pay them off completely and that will be very big problem for you. Also you might not be able to travel where you want to because of weather problems and it destroyed everything but I will tell you how to overcome these roadblocks.

One way you can overcome all of these roadblocks is to ignore all the people in life that try to tear you down just keep walking with your head up and they will wash away like germs. Also when it comes down to hate letters they are just written words so you can take a shredder and shred those letters into a million pieces and go on with your wonderful life. Also bills might get in your way but that won't be a problem because you are successful and successful people get through all of those problems. Last if there is a place you want there is a whole world in front of you just waiting to be explored so why don't you explore it.

Now these are all of my tips for you older self and don't forget them. Also remember that being happy is the key to success in life and happiness will get you far. Be careful older me and don't be too sad when people say mean things they are just words. Be happy and be successful older me and always remember FINISH SCHOOL!!!

Love,

Makaila

-Makaila
Female
7th Grade

The Source to Life

February 27, 2017

Dear Future Ray,

I hope you are living life happily. Hopefully you remember this assignment and know where I'm going with this. My definition of success are my goals, and how to overcome your roadblocks. I hope you know what you are doing in the future. Keep on moving forward. Stay in school. You are smart in 2017. STAY THAT WAY. Accomplish all of your goals, and never give up on them no matter how hard they seem.

What success means to you is what success means to me. Success is accomplishing all of your goals, helping others, have a positive impact on the world. You can be successful by getting a doctorate degree or a PHD, overcome roadblocks, focus on ambitions, or having a good career. Remember to get a nice house or car, and achieve happiness. Lastly, remember to save money and be smart with credit cards.

Now get comfortable because I'm going to explain your goals. Go to U.C.L.A, Harvard, Yale, or Stanford, get a PHD, help the needy, have a good life, and have a family. Remember to have a good marriage, graduate high school as valedictorian of your class , become president, have a good life, don't let anyone tell you can't accomplish your goals Don't forget have a degree, and win the Nobel Prize for World Peace. Lastly, remember to come up with more goals along the road of life.

This is where you need to pay ATTENTION! Now comes your roadblocks and how to overcome them. One roadblock is a heckler, a critic, a non-believer. You can overcome this by not listening to them. Another is the cost of college to get a PHD. Be smart save money, don't go crazy buying stuff.

Lastly, be smart so you can become a future tycoon and have your friends working for you.

Your 12 year old self,

Ray

-Ray
Male
7th Grade

The Source to Life

March 1, 2017

Dear future Paris,

Heyyy girl! So let me give you some ideas to be successful in your life. Success to me is accomplishing your goals. Like getting straight A's and a lot of other things. Also not giving up on anything, just doing your very best in every possible way. Just do your best and never give up on any of your goals and dreams even though it will be tough. Just try harder and harder until you achieve whatever it is you're trying to accomplish.

Now we all know you got some GOALS you want to achieve. So I know that your goals are to be a nurse or doctor, you want to graduate from high school and get your high school diploma. You also you want to graduate college. The college you are thinking of is in Atlanta; either Spelman College or Morehouse College an all black school. You also want to make lots of money. But don't give up I'm telling you you're going to regret it forreal forreal. So just keep going and always think POSITIVE no matter what happens in your life. Take good care of our family even your little sister London even though she is super annoying.

Now you are going to have lots of haters and roadblocks and what I mean is people are going to hate on you no matter what you do if you're popping they going to hate, if you winning they going to hate, if you losing they going to hate anything you do they going to hate so don't trip about what other people think because I never did .So some roadblocks are that you will give up and think negative like that you will give up and stop trying because I'm telling you I have wanted to give up many times but did I not! So just keep going, believe in yourself and DON'T give up. Some more tips are not getting in trouble, staying responsible, always try to go over your standards, and always having good grades. So I hope that you graduate college and go to the college you want to go to and achieve your goals, have good grades, and HAVE FUN while you're going through your life.

Love,

Paris!

Paris
Female
7th Grade

The Source to Life

February 28, 2017

Dear Vanessa,

    I hope you're having a good time in life, and have some successes that are worth telling people! I know high school is getting hard and you feel like you can't do it, but all you have to do is define what "success" means to you. When you were in 7th grade you defined success as being happy, going to a good college, overcoming roadblocks, not worrying about what people said about you and many more! Now, I know they may have changed and you have other goals, but all you have to do is keep your head up and always try your best! If people talk about you, all they want to do is see you fail but you have to keep trying and try your best in everything you do.

    Your goals as a 7th grader, and maybe now, were to help foster kids find a home, get a master's degree, become a singer or a dance teacher, help my family come out of loans they made, save some money so I can get a good house and raise my kids, and many more! As a 7th grader it's pretty tough but I know high school is way harder because you have more classes, you spend more time at school and sometimes you don't like the people in your class. But keep trying and you will reach your goals. If your goals have changed, then I hope they are hard and you can do something with your life while you are working towards your goals. Back then you used to always give up and not try, but now that I know you're in high school and you have friends and more family; I know you can try harder. Now don't think life is all easy because it's not, and here are some reasons why.

Some roadblocks and challenges you are going to face are criticism, getting hurt, not enough money, maybe your grades will drop, family issues, and many more will be thrown your way. A way to overcome these issues and challenges are to try your best never say never, don't give up, always try to find the silver lining in things, save money now,, and always try to keep your grades up to get into a good college! I hope that now that you are a nice, hardworking young lady, you can be something in life and try your best. Always remember to try hard and make friends with the good kids and have a pretty good house and a nice but hard working life job!

Love from 2017,

Vanessa

-Vanessa
Female
7th Grade

The Source to Life

March 25, 2020

Dear Tiana,

Hey girl! Let me tell you everything you need to know about how your life is going to be.

So you want to know about success? Well, here's the thing. Success is just like being confident about everything. It's being able to see your goals and just being happy all the time. Success is just being able to not worry about the bad things people say about you.

Goals. Well, your goals are kind of the same as success. Some of your goals are to go to college and get your doctorate degree. Another goal is to have a good career, to get married and maybe have a few kids…LOL. Your last goal is to accomplish all of your goals.

And last but not least, ROADBLOCKS. Roadblocks are the things that prevent you from achieving your goals. Some roadblocks are haters. Haters can really be annoying sometimes but you'll get used to having haters eventually. To get over roadblocks you just need to ignore it and "keep it moving".

Sincerely,

Tiana

-Tiana
Female
7th Grade

February 28, 2017

Dear Future Self,

Please focus on your dreams like becoming an actor that can act, a rapper that can rap or a singer that can sing. Your personal goal is to get published by the hip-hop magazine, XXL and be the next big thing.

Keep your head up, but not too high. You have so much space left to grow so keep your eyes to the sky, and if we're being real keep your eyes on the prize. Stay focused and negative thoughts will leave your mind. Ignore the haters they don't want to see you on your grind. Never hang out with slackers. They are your main roadblock to becoming an actor or a rapper, it doesn't really matter just make sure to finish school that's the determining factor.

Everybody has a challenge but you have to persevere; you have to stay above average. I know is so hard but just look how you've come so far. You're a rap prodigy and already know what your goals are. Roadblocks/a challenge success is something known as a talent it's rare because it rarely ever happens. You have to achieve your goals no matter what your mind has to say whole because failure is a never ending hole. You need to have strength because the end is far down the road.

With deep regards,
Present Self
Thomas Beeks

-Thomas
Male
7th Grade

The Source to Life

March 1, 2017

Dear future Tanika in 2027,

    My goals in life are not so simple, like I'm worried that I won't be able to do it all in one lifetime. First of all, my real dream is to become an actress because I love to dance and sing, but I want to accomplish other things too. Like I think I want to be a neonatal nurse which is a person that takes care of babies after they're born.

    I think one of my roadblocks will maybe be a financial problem. Some things might be really expensive and I might just give up. Then I tell myself I can't do it, I might just break down. But I know I can overcome them by finding the silver lining of the cloud or to be optimistic. To me that means to find the good in every bad situation. Like I said I want to get my professional degree and I want to be able to pay college tuition for the years I have to be there. I want to go to Harvard or Yale. Those are Ivy League college so you have to have a clean record and that is not easy. I know I have to stay focused and stay true to myself and focus on me.

    I will have haters, right? .So I just need to make haters my motivators .My mom says the best revenge in life is to show them that you made it and are doing better than them. Show them that they can't tear me down and that I did it without them. That no matter what they say or do they are not going to stop me from achieving my dreams and goals. Success to me is to stay focused, to not get distracted and do me stay true to myself.

Sincerely,
Tanika from 2017

-Tanika
Female
7th Grade

February 28, 2017

Dear future self,

Hello, this is you from 2017! I just wanted to say that you have dreams and goals and probably you already succeeded them. But I'm here to give you some tips and advice for your next goals in your life. And to achieve your awesome dreams. Success means to you in 2017 is that you want to visit places like Japan because that's your dream you've said ,or graduate in high school and college or become the world's greatest ,smartest person or even learn a new language which is Japanese and learn new cultures also work at Disneyland cause that's your favorite place and it looks so much fun. I like your goals they are amazing it suits you. And I've heard that you wanted to dye your hair. It's different but I like that. Also I hope you have made it into UCLA because that's the college you wanted to attend when you were my age I guess and probably you made it so congrats.

Let's talk about road blocks because I'm sure you've had them before and now. You probably had them during reaching your goal. Remember that they still come around but that doesn't mean that you should already give up. But you should still move on and ignore the roadblocks and challenges. Of course you're going to get mad and stressed out because I know that you do that and how you are. You're probably too tired to do anything or not able to listen and you have to worry about this and can't do that. So how to overcome those situations are get some inspiration because right now I'm getting inspiration and motivation from social media or even your idols because everyone should have a person to look up to. Ask advice from your family especially your cousin because she has learned a lot when she was facing challenges she would tell you something positive. My last final words that everybody should know is that always try harder and smarter. Until next time, bye!

Sincerely,

Y.M.

-Y.M.
Female
7th Grade

May 27, 2018

Dear future Rosie,

    Hello! This is Rosie from 2017. I know that you are going to be very successful in so many ways. I know that you are going to achieve a lot of your goals. So, here are some things to help you achieve those goals.
    To some people, success means something else. But to me it means to help and care about others. It also means being happy, smart, and achieving your goals as well as overcoming any kinds of challenges you face. And it means to love and care about others.
    We both know that you are going to get a good job and a big house. We also know that we are going to travel all around the world and meet famous people. I also know that you are going to finish school and go to college. So good luck. I hope you will be a good girl.
    But there are going to be some roadblocks ahead of you. You might not have enough money to buy a big house or to travel anywhere in the world. And not getting good grades to finish school. Or finishing school to get a job or have any money. Or not having enough money to pay the bill.
    But there are ways for you to overcome your roadblocks. Like staying in school, then finishing school. Then go to college and graduating with a Master's degree.

Love,
Rosie

p.s. I hope you're doing good in the future.
February 28, 2017

-Rosie
Female
7th Grade

Dear Future Nicholas,

Hi! This is Nicholas from 2017. You are in 7th grade. I know you have a lot of goals you want to accomplish. So, I will tell you some reminders on what certain goals you want to accomplish. As you know, you have always wanted to own at last two Rottweiler dogs. You love to drink apple juice with crackers. And I know you have always wanted to go to UCLA and graduate with a good degree. And you have always wanted to go live in Dallas, Texas right next to the Dallas Cowboys stadium. You probably don't have that much money right now but I know you will get a lot from the career you are going to pick. In seventh grade you really don't know what you are going to be in the future. And I know that you are a very emotional person so you should not give up that easy. Even though these challenges are very tough and may be hard at first, but I know you can do it. One thing that might stop you are the people that get you in gangs or try to make you do drugs. Another challenge that I know you'll accomplish   over is haters. They will haunt you until you fail. So you have to good in life and graduate college.

Sincerely,
Nick

-Nicholas
Male
7th Grade

February 28, 2017

Dear Future Jasmin,

So, you are in your last years of high school. You should have about at least half of your money for college, so I just wanted to encourage you to keep on moving forward. You have been succeeding beautifully in your grades, good job. I hope your mind is still on what 13-year-old Jasmin's mind is on. Let me refresh your mind about what success means to you. To you, success means staying on focused on ambitions, saving enough to make our way through college, and having a positive impact on others.

I love our goals. Oh, I almost forgot, have you accomplished at least half of our goals? Our favorite goal is to go far in our artistic ways. The most important one is to help mom in any way possible. I will go to college and get the highest degree possible, also my favorite. Also getting all A's throughout the school year. Well that's all I have for you regarding that topic, hope you added on to our list of goals and what success is to you.

You must know that there are going to be some challenges/roadblocks ahead that we're going to face. We spotted some, but not all. One was we are having some trouble on making our art go viral. So I figured out a way we can overcome that. We can just practice and practice and look for different ways and opportunities for us to go public. Also have faith and don't stop drawing. Another one was what if we can't make our way through a good college. Well my friend, we have to do is save money...or get good grades so they way is fine too.

So that's all I have for you. Hope you liked our little pep talk. Remember to stay focused and keep trying your best.

Love,

13-year-old Jasmin

-Jasmin
Female
7th Grade

February 7, 2017

Dear Floyd from 2027,

Was the deal? You will have success in many ways.

First you will graduate high school in 2022 then you will get a job until college classes start. When you're at school you will meet a nice girl. You made a commitment to USC. Also you are the starting running back for them. Then at the NFL draft pick you are the first round pick for the Steelers!

People will try to hate on you, hold you down and hold you back but you don't let them. They also try to end your football career but you tend to cut people off.

Your goals in life are to make a millions of dollars playing football. To buy a Bugatti, to live in a mansion, and also to buy your mom a house with a water bed.

Sincerely,

Floyd

-Floyd
Male
7th Grade

August 10, 2030

Dear 19-year-old Israel,

I hope you enjoyed Michigan University. Is your job paying you really good money? You look like you're really successful. Your bachelor's degree looks nice in that frame. Your charity seems to be doing pretty well.

Hope you haven't got hurt in the NFL yet. You should really go out for a ride in your new Lamborghini today. How was Japan, Australia, and the United Kingdom? I hope they were really nice. The mansion must cost you a lot of money. Especially since it's in Long Beach.

School was pretty hard for you. Luckily you studied hard and graduated college. Feeding the kids is costly I bet. But you have an amazing job and you could afford to feed them. Well I'll see you in 5 years.

Sincerely,

23 year old Israel.

-*Israel*
Male
7th Grade

The Source to Life

February 28, 2017

Dear ,

Success is when you go through high school. You'll be getting a job and have a house. Also you will have to go through obstacle in your life like bosses and managers. Don't let others get in your way to success. So that is the way to success.

My goals are to never do bad to others in my school or strangers. My goal is to do good in school in my classes to raise my grades. My goals are to be the best I can be with my skill and my hard work. My goal is to be a pro at basketball in the NBA or be in the Army and the Navy. Lastly, I want to help people in need or that are homeless that's my goal.

My roadblocks are sometimes just me when I get lazy. I sometimes have to go somewhere when I get home. I will sometimes follow other people's lead on something I don't know. When I talk to someone when I'm not supposed to. I'll sometimes get distracted by something or someone. What I can do to overcome my roadblocks is to not give into them.

Sincerely,

-Anonymous
7th Grade

September 13, 2021

Dear 13 year-old

Hello younger self! I know right now you just want to give up and throw everything away. But don't, because if you do you will regret it. You will look back and wonder why you were being so harsh on yourself.

This is how we accomplish our goals. We graduate from middle school, and those were the worst years of our life. We are about to graduate high school. We are so smart we graduated all four years with honor roll. We graduate from high school from Paraclete High School. We kept our friends positive, many friends went left on us but others stayed right. The main person who stuck by our side was Chanay, unlike everyone she's a true friend!

Our goals are to graduate high school, go to college, graduate college, get our doctorate degree and be the best Pediatric doctor ever! I'm pretty sure we're going to achieve those last two. Why wouldn't we? We're awesome. Another goal we have is to meet Candace Parker. Our last goal is to just make it, honestly. We strive to be the best at something, almost anything.

Basketball life was pretty crazy, it wasn't easy. We had a lot of hate, a lot. And with injuries in our way we were pretty sad. So we had to give up on ball for a while. So after a while our knees got stronger. We never gave up on nursing. Nursing school is a long so be prepared for your journey.

Sincerely your favorite person,
17 year old

-*Anonymous*
Female
7th Grade

February 28, 2017

Dear future ,

    Hey future me, how is life going for you? I hope you are doing good and, that you are very successful. Don't worry about anything but success because it's all you'll ever need in life. It'll also help you with everything, like if you were to graduate college, which is a part of success, various amount of opportunities will come your way. Success to me is basically achieving goals and becoming something and not be one of those people just lying on the couch at home watching TV all day.

    I feel like the only thing that can become a roadblock for me is myself. Like when I get mad I don't know how to control myself. Also, I have a poor attitude and, a lot of times it gets me in trouble. I can overcome those roadblocks though if really try my best. Also, I can just try to do things that help me get better hopefully I did and, I was a success in life.

    My goals in life are kind of easy but, at the same time hard. My goal is to simply be something in life. I grew up with having no one in my family graduate from college and, I want to break that chain. I want to be the first person to graduate from college so I can be a good example for all of the younger kids in my family.

Sincerely,

                                                       -*Anonymous*
                                                       Female
                                                       7th Grade

February 28, 2035

Dear ██████ in 2017

Success is something when nothing gets in your way. Success is when each day is a great day. When you're successful nothing will ever get in your way. If you have a happy life you will never ever complain. At the age of thirty-five you will have really a nice life with a really nice wife. She will always make you food and you will always be in a good mood. You will start success at the age of twenty. Also, Brandon don't worry about money because you will have plenty.

██████, I hope you are having fun achieving all of your goals. I remember how nothing ever got in your way since you were twelve years old. Remember how you went to jail for breaking through security? Trying to meet your favorite soccer player. Seriously, that was a bad idea you could have done it better. At least you're going to be friends with him and that's all that matters. Don't be bad, be good. Also I know getting good grades is something you would do.

As you get older it will be tougher. Don't worry about roadblocks, you will get past them. Sometimes you will have trouble financially but you will make it so keep hustling. Roadblocks are something you will get past. So don't worry about them and just work fast.

Sincerely,

███

-Anonymous

Male

7th Grade

February 28, 2024

Dear ▮▮▮▮ in 2017,

    Hi, how are you? We are now in 2024, you are now 18-years-old and you made it to college. Hey, I know that you are doing what success means to you and I just wanted to tell you that you have done a great job on defining what success means to you. So I just wanted to tell you that when you are defining success it is not all about being happy. I'm not saying that you can't be happy doing this things because you can. But it is more about staying focused, having positive thoughts, not letting people distract you and your impacts. It is also about doing right in class and staying on top of your school work because it gets harder every grade level. Hey, just to let you know that you are a very nice girl and you managed to get a 4.0 in all your classes. Keep it up.

    Now, let's get into what your goals are. Just to let you know, I am going to tell you which ones have come true so far. You said that you wanted to take care of your parents, which is true. The next one is that you wanted to get into Harvard. Also, to stay close to your family and play basketball. Keep setting goals. They WILL come true.

    These are the ways that you will overcome roadblocks. One is that you always studied. Second, is that you do not get in to every ones business anymore. Third is that you do not talk back. Also that you are not getting mad so easily.

    Sincerely,
    ▮▮▮▮

-*Anymous*
Female
7th Grade

The Choice

This not a game because no one is going to

help you

this is not a game so don't mess it all up,

Or you will get road blocks you will get money

that means no education

that means no graduation,

This is not a game because no one is going to

help you

this is not a game so don't mess it all up.

The only way to overcome them is to stay out of trouble,

get good grades to graduate so you can get a house and a job now,

This is not a game so no one is going to help you

this is not a game so don't mess it all up.

-Anonymous
Male
7th Grade

CHAPTER 3

MR. BERMAN

COMPASSION,

One of my goals for the future is to become a manga artist or make anime shows. For this passage we will be talking about compassion. A role of compassion that I would do for my future is give people extraordinary mangas and anime shows. I would like to be compassionate with these things because these are my talents. My real talent is drawing and watching anime is something I like to do when i'm bored. So why not draw anime and make books or shows out of the characters I draw. These are the main things I can be compassionate at. like for instance when I make my manga I can give to people by being compassionate. My success would not be successful without compassion because you have to talk nice and don't be rude when you do it. If you are rude when you do it you might get sued or even go to jail. Here's a reason of what I can do to make my business successful I can give people nice comments then they might give me nice comments about my art or show. When you get more nice comments you will have a better way of being more famous or you might even get paid more. So pretty much what I'm trying to say is that having compassion will make you more noticeable or have more friends.

-D.W.
Male
8th grade

What is the hardest goal to achieve?

Everyone has their own achievements, but we also have
difficult goals we want to improve and overcome in life. I really want to improve on never giving up during the hardest times. I usually start giving up when something becomes difficult because I don't believe I could do it. I need to believe in myself more or else I'll fail at everything. No one should ever give up or feel as if no one believes in them. I want to graduate from school and say I never gave up because I actually had faith in myself. I need to improve on never giving up because I'll feel better about myself and do better. You shouldn't be scared whenever life gets difficult then you'll give up. I will try with all my power to overcome my goal on not giving up in life ever.

-Daniela
Female
8th grade

Dreams Of Fame

    I think I will stay by my motivation which is no thought no goal, no goal no gold, and no gold no mold (of myself) and stay on the path you're supposed to be on. My main goal is to become a comedian/ actor because I'm the best at it. But to do that I need to complete school and get all the hard things done first and then I can get to the easy things like acting, oh and I'll do art, I'll be that one famous person that does a lot of things but if none of that happens, I'll become a youtuber because some youtubers be in movies so there is a chance i would be in a movie..... I hope. See I have many goals that I want to complete but only some will get done. There will be things that will try to stop you though, so you gotta find your through, and if you have trouble there will always be people that will help you and they will complete goals with you, so there is many compassion things people do and help you with and that is awesome because no matter how hard it looks you can always get past it, No matter how tall or strong it is. So if I complete all my goals and get through all the hard things I'll be on the T.V. in no time and in movies and I'll live a good life YA-DIGGG

Cameron
8th Grade

The good and bad

Everyone has their good and bad. To be a better (you), you should work on the negative. I have goals that I want to accomplish, but I know I can't make it if I have a bad attitude. That's one of my main negative characteristics. People tell me all the time, they say you can be great you just need to keep your emotions and attitude in check. The reason I care about this problem the most is because I know this is true. I can become something but it all starts with the little things. To be honest, the reason I think it's difficult is because when I let people get to me and take over my whole day, I bring all that anger and sadness to whatever I'm doing or take it out on something or someone else. That's something I need to work on. If I don't overcome this I won't be able to accomplish anything in life. This is one of my characteristics I need to work on to become more successful.

-Amina
Female
8th Grade

Daryl's Anthology Project

First of all my goal is to go to Japan because of a certain president. I'd tell you my dreams but when I wake up I forget so my bad. Challenges I have to defeat to go to Japan are: getting into college (because if you do you'll most likely get good grades) then get a good job, get a bunch of money, then get three tickets to go to Japan. Then I will read a lot of Naruto manga and the three tickets are for me Daniel and Cameron they will have to buy their own tickets of course.

-Daryl
Male
8th Grade

The most exciting part of my future?

The most exciting part of my future pathway is graduating from college. Why? Because I want to graduate so I can say I did it. I look forward to it the most because I want to graduate from college and get a good job. First I have to finish middle school and high school. But by that I have to do right in class, have good grades, and work hard plus I have to do the same in high school. What do I have to do to get there? Well, I have to listen and learn, I have to have good grades, and I have to do my best and believe in myself.

Another exciting part of my future is having a job when I get older. I look forward to it the most because it's going to help me. In other words, it helps me make money and money helps me get nice things in life. I have to go to college and graduate in order for me to get a job and it's a lot more things to do. This is my statement on the most exciting part of my future.

-Donnae
Female
8th Grade

Do you see yourself walking a compassionate path?

Yes, I do see myself walking a compassionate path to my goals and future. If I'm not compassionate along the way then i know I wouldn't get anywhere. It's just like having respect to others and for yourself. I have personal goals, it will lead me to a better future. My goal is to be a nurse and be a sign language teacher and if I'm not compassionate I won't be able to be those things. So I do see myself walking a compassionate path. I also want to show my family and the close ones I made it and I'm successful. I also want my future to be successful so I can show all the people that hate me and talk down on me that i am doing great without them.

-Domonique
Female
8th Grade

My definition of success

My definition of success is: getting a scholarship to Paraclete high. It will be very tough but I know if I work hard like I am now I can get into Paraclete high and get through it. I also want to play for Paracletes basketball team and win a champion. Then I want to get a scholarship to either UCLA or OREGON for college(depends on if I play basketball or football). Then in college I want to get my masters degree and finish at the top of my class and hopefully I could get drafted into the NBA for my favorite team the Los Angeles Lakers or to the NFL for the San Francisco 49ers. When I'm in the NBA I want to become a great legend like Kobe, Jordan or Lebron but better and make it into the Hall of Fame after becoming a legend.

-Jamerius
Male
8th Grade

THE DIFFICULT KEY

The most difficult and struggling key for me is how to achieve at what I want to be in or do in life. The reason why I think that is the most struggling key for me is there is always an obstacle that cut me off at my path/road to success. When I see a road block I feel the need to **STOP** because that little block or wall is in my way. I think that the bigger it gets the more I hesitate. It is a challenge for me because the whole time I think that not achieving is the easiest thing but, it's actually the hardest because you're failing in yourself. I think that not achieving in something that you really want to be in life is good but, someone told me it's not because when you don't achieve in anything, you fail and everything that you work hard for is gone and will never come back.. Someone once told me that when you push yourself to your limit you think it's hard, but actually it's not unless you make it hard. Every day I think that I can't overcome that one road block that is blocking my path/road to success because of how much I don't take "life" serious my mom once said, but now I know that the one and only **KEY** on my ring, is the **KEY** that blows away all of the roadblocks in my life and path/road to success.

-Jay
Male
8th grade

MY KEY TO SUCCESS

My key to success is to : focus. It's hard for me to focus a lot of the time. For me, it's sometimes out of laziness. And there are a lot of people that lose. Focus because of school (as most kids tend to go to school just for fun). Or just to see their boyfriend or their friends. That can really pull you away from what you're coming to school for which is to learn. And then, when people get put back a grade they become mad. honestly mainly i lose focus a lot and i come to school because of my friends. A lot of the times i don't even go to school because i think its boring. But now i know i still have to come so i can be successful in life. So so that's why anybody going through the same thing, they should keep going to school and keep their head up. Also, my key to success is: is to not give in to what people say about me or what people think about me. Ignore the drama because it's not worth it. People just want to make you mad. I prefer to not live off of the hype. And focus on school. And yes you can got to school and have fun but you still have to do work. Truthfully, that part is the hardest for me to do. But, i have to realize that i only have me, in this world. I'm going to have my own back when no one does at the end of it all.

-Siaryha
Female
8th Grade

What is the most difficult place for you to attain success in ?

The most difficult place for me to attain success in is
achieving most of my goals,
Simply because I struggle really, really hard to keep
My grades up to A's and that has been
My goal.

Aside from that main goal,
I have other goals that are important to me too,
Such as my top goal of becoming a singer
For a career.

Singing is just what I love to do,
Being a praise dancer and other things also
Matter too.
As I go through my school life and achieve
That one goal of getting all A's but,
While i'm achieving my goals in school
I'm not at all practicing my other few goals.

My parents want me to be a straight A
Student and that's what i'm doing
While i'm still in school,
But I practice on my other goals,
At home (becoming a singer) but
Every time I try to do that my Auntie
Asks me to stop so I wonder sometimes....

Will I ever achieve my dream ?
Honestly being a singer is my biggest dream and

I know some people say i've got a long way to go but I want
To start now.

I know that when becoming a singer you
Still need good grades.
I don't want to be a singer
And be dumb,
Because no one will ever
Sign you like that.

Now, we all know getting straight A's
Is not easy
But you have to at least try even
If the struggle is real and since it is so real
The struggle should motivate you to
Work harder and harder.

Keep coming back stronger and stronger,
But also remember to do what makes you
Happy and not what your
Forced to do

-Malaijah
Female
8th Grade

The Source to Life

The most difficult subject for me is math. It's not easy to do. Most of the time I don't like math because it's so difficult. Trying to do math even though it is hard. Is one key to success in my life I can ask for help with my math. Talking to the class is also hard for me because I'm shy. I want to talk to them but I can't. I try to talk to them more. This is one of my keys to success. Drawing is a little difficult for me. I ask Mr.Finney for help so I can go to an art school. I don't like going school but I know that I have to go school. School is going to help me be successful in my life so I can get a job so I can have money for a home and a cat.

-Kelly
8th Grade

MY DOOR TO SUCCESS

When my road is finally over, I will have all the keys that I have worked for. Then I can turn them into a big key so I can open my door and uncover a new road that I have to cover. All I ever wanted is the success that some of my family never got. For example my dad, all he got as success is finishing high school. He does not want me and my brother to end up like him. Also, he does not want my brother and I to get a lazy job that everyone can get just for finishing high school. What he wants from me and my brother is to get a career that anybody can get without working physically hard. I promised him that I will reach to the door that was made for me and go through it and beyond. I will prove to anybody that said or says that I cannot make it and achieve it.

- *Valeria G.*
Female
8th grade

CHAPTER 4

MS. GROSE
(HIGH SCHOOL)

The Source to Life

4/5//2017

    The key to success is patience; it is the ability to tolerate trouble or suffering without getting irritated or upset. Patience is an important, yet complex quality to have, trait in life that one must have in order to get through the reality of the world. We all have to go through many obstacles that we wish we did not have to go through whether it being standing in line to order your food or simply having to ignore impolite comments. We all have an image in our head of a goal, but it always gets waved away when we do not have the patience to focus on the positivity and what we want. We automatically become sailing boats and slowly drift away from our goals due to the negativity of someone's words or actions. My goal is to become a crime scene investigator, but my father wasn't so fond of the idea and never gives me the support I wish I had. Instead I receive a pessimistic attitude and a comment on how he does not believe I will achieve my goal. To overcome this challenge in my life, I have decided that I will ignore his hopeless words and prove him that I can. Do not give up and have the virtue of patience, ignore the rude comments and pass the obstacles in life in order to reach your goal.

Angelina
Female
9th Grade

Keys to Success

What does it take to be successful?

The key to success is to do what you think is best. Now, I'm not saying to rob a bank to be rich or anything, but go with what you know is good for you. I personally believe that going to college for the career you want is successful. I don't think you should go to college to do what your parents tell you to do, because you won't be happy about it. You may have some challenges along the way, such as depression, financial issues, but with determination and perseverance, you can make it! Good luck!

Alexis
Female
9th Grade

The Keys To Success

The keys to success. Being successful means actually wanting what you are trying to achieve. To have a successful career your intentions and attitude on getting to your destination have to be pure. If you are only doing something for the money or all the wrong reasons that's not getting you anywhere. Being successful or the process of getting successful isn't always easy. If you really want something try your hardest to get it. Challenge your limits, don't limit your challenges. Honestly sometimes being successful comes easy, but that's only sometimes. Also it is very important for you to be yourself at all times. Walk and talk with confidence. Acting a certain way to get a certain place isn't a good idea. It will start to wear off and the real you will show. In the movie Kung Fu Panda 3, master Shifu said to Po, "If you only do what you can do, you will never be more that what you are." Strive to do better and be better in every way. Dreams don't work unless you do. Reaching that goal that you've been trying to reach is a very great feeling. In the end we only regret the chances we didn't take. Live your life to the fullest. Don't let people or your life lessons slow you down. People will hate you, rate you, shake you, break you, but how strong you stand is what makes you. Stop using the word "can't" take that word out your vocabulary box, ball it up, throw is on the floor, and stump on it. If you want it, go get it. If you have it, appreciate it. Your decisions you make now are what hold your future. Also stay positive and do the best you can. Extend the possibilities by taking risks every once in awhile. Don't be afraid to be outgoing. Remember, the past is your lesson, the present is your gift, and the future is your motivation.

~ Niah
Female
9th Grade

Autographs

Autographs

Autographs

Autographs

Autographs

Affirmative Expression would like to congratulate the Life Source Scholars for completing

The Anthology Project

and earning the prestigious title of *published authors!*

If you would like to bring **The Anthology Project** to your school, church, program, or organization please contact us!

Affirmative Expression's
Anthology Project
Turning your students into authorpreneurs!
Tierica Berry (Founder)
678.499.4405

Info@AffirmativeExpression.com
www.AffirmativeExpression.com

www.ingramcontent.com/pod-product-compliance
Lightning Source LLC
Chambersburg PA
CBHW071716040426
42446CB00011B/2084